CANADA 2016 HUMAN RIGHTS REPORT

EXECUTIVE SUMMARY

Canada is a constitutional monarchy with a federal parliamentary government. In a free and fair multiparty federal election held in October 2015, the Liberal Party, led by Justin Trudeau, won a majority of seats in the federal parliament and formed a government.

Civilian authorities maintained effective control over the security forces.

The principal human rights problems included violence against women, disparities in living conditions between indigenous and nonindigenous peoples, and trafficking in persons.

The government took steps to investigate, prosecute, and punish all officials who committed violations, whether in the security forces or elsewhere in the government.

Section 1. Respect for the Integrity of the Person, Including Freedom from:

a. Arbitrary Deprivation of Life and other Unlawful or Politically Motivated Killings

There were no reports the government or its agents committed arbitrary or unlawful killings.

b. Disappearance

There were no reports of politically motivated disappearances.

c. Torture and Other Cruel, Inhuman, or Degrading Treatment or Punishment

The law prohibits such practices, and there were no reports that government officials employed them.

Prison and Detention Center Conditions

There were no significant reports regarding prison or detention center conditions that raised human rights concerns.

Physical Conditions: According to the governmental statistical agency's most recent figures, in 2014-15 there were on average approximately 39,625 inmates, pretrial detainees, and remand prisoners in federal and provincial correctional institutions, which had an official capacity of 38,771. The remand population exceeded the sentenced population. The national double-bunking rate (the practice of confining two inmates in a cell designed for one) in federal facilities was 19 percent in 2013-14.

The federal correctional investigator's report for 2014-15 identified recourse to "administrative segregation" or solitary confinement by federal correctional services to manage crowded institutions and high-needs inmates as a concern. The correctional investigator, an independent prison ombudsman, urged authorities to cap the time inmates spend in segregation and to develop a policy framework to guide the use of segregation, including prohibiting the use of long-term segregation (beyond 15 days) for inmates with mental disabilities. Correctional Services Canada reported that the number of federal inmates held in solitary confinement for 120 days or more fell from 498 to 247 (a 51 percent drop) from March 2015 to March 2016, in part due to diversion of inmates with mental disabilities to treatment programs as an alternative to segregation.

In May the Ontario ombudsman recommended the government end the practice of extended solitary confinement in provincial prisons. The ombudsman's report also recommended prison personnel receive training on the mental health effects of long-term solitary confinement and legislated maximums for periods of solitary confinement.

In October the Ontario provincial government transferred an indigenous prisoner out of solitary confinement after he spent more than 1,500 consecutive days in a cell under continuous artificial light for 23 hours each day while awaiting trial. Ontario's Human Rights Commissioner flagged this case to prison authorities who then moved the man to a different cell. In October the Ontario Minister of Community Safety and Correctional Services announced a 15- day limit on the number of consecutive days inmates can be held in solitary confinement (down from the present 30-day guideline), effective immediately. The minister also announced that each detention facility would establish segregation committees that would meet weekly and review the cases of prisoners in solitary confinement. The minister said jails should use solitary confinement as a measure of last resort under the least restrictive conditions available and ordered an independent review of policies and practices in Ontario jails. Advocates for prisoners said the changes were insufficient.

The Correctional Investigator's Office reported 10 nonnatural deaths (including suicide) in federal custody in 2014-15, the latest available figures.

In July the government of New Brunswick announced it would advise the public when a prisoner dies but would not publish details on the inmate's death. The change came after media reported 13 persons had died in New Brunswick prisons since 2004, but the coroner reviewed only four of the deaths.

In August the families of two female inmates who died in a Nova Scotia prison filed suit against the federal government for wrongful death. The families alleged prison authorities were negligent in addressing mental health needs of the inmates, both of whom committed suicide in 2015 after stints in solitary confinement.

Administration: Independent authorities investigated credible allegations of inhuman behavior and documented the results of such investigations in a publicly accessible manner.

Independent Monitoring: The government permitted visits by independent nongovernmental human rights observers.

d. Arbitrary Arrest or Detention

The law prohibits arbitrary arrest and detention, and the government generally observed these prohibitions.

Role of the Police and Security Apparatus

National, provincial, and municipal police forces maintain internal security. The armed forces are responsible for external security but in exceptional cases may exercise some domestic security responsibility at the formal request of civilian provincial authorities. The federal Royal Canadian Mounted Police (RCMP) reports to the Department of Public Safety, and the armed forces report to the Department of National Defense. Provincial and municipal police report to their respective provincial authorities. The Canada Border Services Agency reports to the Department of Public Safety and Emergency Preparedness and is responsible for enforcing immigration law. Civilian authorities maintained effective control over the RCMP and provincial and municipal police forces, and the government has effective mechanisms to investigate and punish abuse and corruption. There were no reports of impunity involving the security forces during the year. Authorities investigated and publicly reported all fatalities that resulted from police action or in police custody.

Arrest Procedures and Treatment of Detainees

Authorities generally apprehended persons openly with warrants. A judge can issue a warrant after being satisfied a criminal offense might have been committed. A person arrested for a criminal offense has the right to a prompt, independent judicial determination of the legality of the detention. Authorities respected this right in practice. Authorities provided detainees with timely information of the reason for the arrest and ensured prompt access to a lawyer of the detainee's choice or, if the detainee was indigent, a lawyer provided by the state without restriction. Bail generally was available. Suspects were not detained incommunicado or held under house arrest.

Judges may issue preemptive peace bonds and apprehend individuals who authorities reasonably believe may carry out terrorist activities. Judges may also issue recognizances to detain persons and impose bail conditions if authorities deem the restrictions likely to prevent terrorist activity. Authorities may hold persons under preventive detention under recognizance for up to seven days, subject to periodic judicial review. Restrictions may include limits on travel and surrender of passports. Use of peace bonds and recognizance for counterterrorism purposes is subject to annual reporting requirements to the federal parliament.

Pretrial Detention: Authorities released detainees immediately after they were charged, unless a judge deemed continued detention necessary to ensure the detainee's attendance in court, for the protection or safety of the public, or due to the gravity of the offense. Persons subject to continued detention have the right to judicial review of their status at regular intervals.

The government may detain or deport noncitizens on national security grounds with an immigration security certificate. The government issues certificates based on confidential evidence presented to two cabinet ministers by intelligence or police agencies and reviewed by a federal court judge who determines "reasonableness" and upholds or revokes the certificate. A judge may order an individual detained during the security certificate determination process if the government believes the individual presents a danger to national security or is unlikely to appear at the proceeding for removal. The judge may impose conditions on release into the community, including monitoring. Individuals subject to a security certificate may see a summary of confidential evidence against them. Authorities must provide full disclosure to court-appointed, security-cleared lawyers (special advocates), who can review and challenge the evidence on behalf of these individuals but not share or discuss the material with them. The law establishes strict rules on the disclosure and use of secret evidence, prohibits the use of evidence if there are reasonable grounds to believe authorities obtained the evidence as a result of torture, and provides mechanisms for review and appeal.

Detainee's Ability to Challenge Lawfulness of Detention before a Court: Persons arrested or detained are entitled to challenge in court the validity of the detention and to obtain prompt release and compensation if the detention is found to be unlawful.

e. Denial of Fair Public Trial

The law provides for an independent judiciary, and the government generally respected judicial independence.

Trial Procedures

The law provides for the right to a fair public trial, and an independent judiciary generally enforced this right. Trials are held without undue delay before a judge alone or, for more serious cases, before a judge and jury. Defendants have the right to be present at trial and to consult with an attorney of their choice in a timely manner. The government provides an attorney at public expense if needed when defendants face serious criminal charges, and defendants may confront or question witnesses against them and present witnesses and evidence on their behalf. Defendants and their attorneys generally have access to government-held evidence relevant to their cases and adequate time and facilities to prepare a defense. Defendants also enjoy a presumption of innocence, a right to be informed promptly and in detail of the charges against them (with free interpretation as necessary from the moment charged through all appeals), a right not to be compelled to testify or confess guilt, and a right of appeal. The law extends these rights to all citizens.

Political Prisoners and Detainees

There were no reports of political prisoners or detainees.

Civil Judicial Procedures and Remedies

There is an independent and impartial judiciary in civil matters and access to a court to bring a suit seeking damages for, or cessation of, a human rights violation. Remedies can be monetary, declaratory, or injunctive. Federal or provincial human rights commissions may also hear alleged human rights violations. Individuals may also bring human rights complaints to the UN or the Inter-American Commission on Human Rights.

f. Arbitrary or Unlawful Interference with Privacy, Family, Home, or Correspondence

The law prohibits such actions, and there were no reports that the government failed to respect these prohibitions.

Section 2. Respect for Civil Liberties, Including:

a. Freedom of Speech and Press

The constitution and law provide for freedom of speech and press, and the government generally respected these rights. An independent press, an effective judiciary, and a functioning democratic political system combined to promote freedom of speech and press.

Freedom of Speech and Expression: The Supreme Court has ruled that the government may limit free speech in the name of goals such as ending discrimination, ensuring social harmony, or promoting gender equality. The court has also ruled that the benefits of limiting hate speech and promoting equality are sufficient to outweigh the freedom of speech clause in the Charter of Rights and Freedoms, the country's constitutional bill of rights.

The criminal code prohibits public incitement and willful promotion of hatred against an identifiable group in any medium. Inciting hatred (in certain cases) or genocide is a criminal offense, but the Supreme Court sets a high threshold for such cases, specifying that these acts must be proven to be willful and public. Provincial-level film censorship, broadcast licensing procedures, broadcasters' voluntary codes curbing graphic violence, and laws against hate literature and pornography impose some restrictions on the media.

In November media reported that municipal and provincial police in Quebec had electronically monitored seven journalists in the province on multiple occasions between 2008 and 2016. In each case the police had a warrant from a Quebec court authorizing the surveillance. The most recent case started in 2016 as police investigated an internal leak suggesting police officers may have fabricated evidence. The electronic monitoring allowed police authorities to track the journalists' movements and telephone logs. Federal, Quebec, and Montreal politicians condemned the electronic surveillance. The provincial government of Quebec committed to make it more difficult for police to obtain warrants to monitor journalists, and it launched a public commission to investigate the incidents. The commission's investigation had not started as of November 8.

In July the Quebec Human Rights Tribunal ordered a comedian to pay C$42,000 ($32,400) to the family of a child whose appearance he mocked during a stand-up routine. The judge determined the comedian's joke did not qualify as protected speech and violated the child's right to protection against discriminatory comments. In October the Quebec Court of Appeals granted the comedian permission to file an appeal.

Internet Freedom

The government did not restrict or disrupt access to the internet or censor online content, and there were no credible reports that the government monitored private online communications without appropriate legal authority.

Approximately 99 percent of households could access broadband services. According to the World Bank, 87 percent of the population used the internet in 2014.

Academic Freedom and Cultural Events

There were no government restrictions on academic freedom or cultural events.

b. Freedom of Peaceful Assembly and Association

The law provides for the freedoms of assembly and association, and the government generally respected these rights.

c. Freedom of Religion

See the Department of State's *International Religious Freedom Report* at
www.state.gov/religiousfreedomreport/.

d. Freedom of Movement, Internally Displaced Persons, Protection of Refugees, and Stateless Persons

The constitution and law provide for freedom of internal movement, foreign travel, emigration, and repatriation, and the government generally respected these rights.

The government cooperated with the Office of the UN High Commissioner for Refugees and other humanitarian organizations in providing protection and assistance to internally displaced persons, refugees, returning refugees, asylum seekers, stateless persons, and other persons of concern.

Protection of Refugees

Access to Asylum: The law provides for the granting of asylum or refugee status, and the government has established a system for providing protection to refugees. The government offered alternatives to refugee claimants whose cases the Immigration and Refugee Board (IRB) refused. The option for judicial review through the federal courts exists. Two other remedies of last resort are available through the Department of Immigration, Refugees, and Citizenship: a "preremoval risk assessment" and an appeal to the minister of immigration, refugees, and citizenship for a waiver based on humanitarian and compassionate grounds.

In January the government dropped its appeal of a 2015 court ruling that found authorities' denial of access to appeal by refugee claimants from designated countries of origin (DCOs) was unconstitutional. DCOs include countries that do not normally produce refugees but respect human rights and offer state protection, or countries whose nationals have a high rate of rejection by the IRB and regularly abandon or withdraw asylum claims in Canada.

Claimants who arrive in the country in a manner designated by the minister as a mass or irregular arrival (in cases of suspected human smuggling) may be subject to detention (subject to review at legislated intervals) pending verification of their identity and admissibility. They face restrictions on access to appeal and remedies of last resort if the IRB refuses their claims.

Durable Solutions: The government accepted refugees for resettlement from third countries and facilitated local integration (including naturalization), particularly of refugees in protracted situations. The government assisted the safe, voluntary return of refugees to their homes.

Temporary Protection: The government also provided temporary protection (in the form of temporary residence permits) to persons who may not qualify as refugees.

Section 3. Freedom to Participate in the Political Process

The law provides citizens the ability to choose their government in free and fair periodic elections held by secret ballot and based on universal and equal suffrage.

Elections and Political Participation

Recent Elections: In October 2015 the Liberal Party won a majority of seats in the federal parliament and formed a national government following a free and fair election.

Participation of Women and Minorities: No laws limit the participation of women or minorities in the political process, and they did participate. In November 2015 Prime Minister Trudeau named his cabinet, which, for the first time in the country's history, included an equal number of men and women.

Section 4. Corruption and Lack of Transparency in Government

The law provides criminal penalties for corruption by officials, and the government generally implemented the law effectively. There were isolated reports of government corruption during the year.

Corruption: In December former Laval Mayor Gilles Vaillancourt pleaded guilty to charges of fraud, breach of trust, and conspiracy to commit fraud, after running one of Quebec's largest cities for 23 years. He agreed to repay illicit gains and forfeit assets worth C$8.5 million ($6.5 million). Vaillancourt could face up to six years in prison.

Prosecutors dropped fraud and related charges against Senator Patrick Brazeau and a judge dismissed charges against Senator Mike Duffy; the Senate reinstated both members. Prosecutors also dropped charges against former Senator Mac Harb and police terminated the investigation into official expenses claimed by Senator Pamela Wallin.

In November 2015 Quebec's Charbonneau Commission released its final report of its investigation into the awarding of public construction projects. The report concluded corruption in the province's construction sector was widespread and made 60 recommendations for major reforms to Quebec's public contracts system.

<u>Financial Disclosure</u>: By law public officeholders, including elected members of the executive branch and their staff and designated senior nonelected officials, must disclose information about their personal financial assets. These declarations, as well as an annual report, are available to the public through regular reports from a commissioner for conflict of interest and ethics. The commissioner may impose an administrative monetary penalty for noncompliance, but the law does not provide for criminal sanctions. Members of the legislative branch are not required to disclose financial holdings but must recuse themselves from voting or conducting hearings on matters in which they have a pecuniary interest. Provincial governments provide independent audits of government business and ombudsman services.

<u>Public Access to Information</u>: The law permits public access to government information, and the government granted access for citizens and noncitizens, including foreign media. The law provides for the denial of legal requests for information on limited and specific grounds given and cited in law, a reasonably short timeline to disclose or respond, reasonable processing fees, and a mechanism to appeal denials, including appeal to the federal courts. The law does not impose criminal or administrative sanctions for noncompliance. The government released quarterly information on the public expenditures of senior government officials and published expense information on individual ministerial websites and a centralized website.

In May the government announced it would charge only a nominal C$5.00 ($3.80) application fee to request federal records and eliminate all other fees. The government also announced reforms to allow requesters to specify the format for data, making it easier for users to sort and analyze government data.

Section 5. Governmental Attitude Regarding International and Nongovernmental Investigation of Alleged Violations of Human Rights

A wide variety of domestic and international human rights groups generally operated without government restriction, investigating and publishing their findings on human rights cases. Government officials were cooperative and responsive to their views.

<u>Government Human Rights Bodies</u>: Federal and provincial human rights commissions enjoyed government cooperation, operated without government or party interference, and had adequate resources. Observers considered the commissions effective. Parliamentary human rights committees operated in the House of Commons and the Senate. The committees acted independently of government, conducted public hearings, and issued reports and recommendations to which the government provided written, public, and timely responses. Most federal departments and some federal agencies employed ombudsmen. Nine provinces and one territory also employed ombudsmen.

The Truth and Reconciliation Commission (TRC) on Indian Residential Schools released its full report in November 2015 (see section 6, Indigenous People), and the federal government launched a national inquiry into missing and murdered indigenous women (see section 6, Women).

Section 6. Discrimination, Societal Abuses, and Trafficking in Persons

Women

<u>Rape and Domestic Violence</u>: The law criminalizes rape, including spousal rape, as sexual assault, and the government enforced the law effectively. Penalties for sexual assault carry sentences of up to 10 years in prison, up to 14 years for sexual assault with a restricted or prohibited firearm, and between four years and life for aggravated sexual assault with a firearm or committed for the benefit of, at the direction of, or in association with, a criminal organization. According to the government's statistical agency, in 2015 police received approximately 21,500 reports of sexual assault, sexual assault with a weapon or causing bodily harm, and aggravated sexual assault (up from 20,735 in 2014). Most victims were women. Government studies indicated victims of sexual assault reported approximately one in 20 incidents to police. The federal government does not publish statistics on the number of abusers prosecuted, convicted, and punished.

The law prohibits domestic violence. Although the criminal code does not define specific domestic violence offenses, an abuser can be charged with an applicable offense, such as assault, aggravated assault, intimidation, mischief, or sexual assault. Persons convicted of assault receive up to five years in prison. Assaults involving weapons, threats, or injuries carry terms of up to 10 years. Aggravated assault or endangerment of life carry prison sentences of up to 14 years. The government enforced the law effectively. Studies indicated that victims of domestic violence and spousal abuse underreported incidents, likely due to social stigma or fear of further violence or retribution.

According to the government's statistical agency, indigenous women were three times more likely than nonindigenous women to experience violent abuse and, according to the RCMP, were four times more likely to be victims of homicide. In June 2015 the RCMP reported indigenous women were disproportionately represented as victims of homicide and in missing persons cases. The report found there were 204 unresolved cases involving the disappearance or homicide of indigenous women, a decrease from 225 in 2014. A 2014 RCMP report concluded 1,017 indigenous women had been killed between 1980 and 2012 and that another 164 were missing. Civil society representatives and government officials said the number of cases may be much higher and alleged there were irregularities in investigations of the disappearances and killings of indigenous women. Civil society groups also claimed the government failed to allocate adequate resources to address these cases.

In August the federal government launched a national inquiry into the issue of missing and murdered indigenous women. Five independent commissioners were directed to investigate and produce a public report of their findings by the end of 2018. The government conducted preinquiry consultations with indigenous stakeholders throughout the country and defined the inquiry's terms of reference. The government provided C$53.8 million ($41.3 million) to fund the inquiry.

In November the Quebec provincial government, citing insufficient evidence, announced it would not lay charges against nine provincial police officers related to allegations in 2015 by indigenous women in the northwestern Quebec community of Val d'Or that the officers sexually assaulted them, gave them money and drugs for sexual services, physically abused them, or drove them out of town in the winter and forced them to walk home in the cold. An independent observer appointed by the government concluded the investigation was fair and impartial but called for consultations between indigenous communities and the province.

The government's statistical agency reported there were 627 shelters and transition homes providing services to abused women. Shelters provided emergency care, transition housing, counseling, and referrals to legal and social service agencies. Some shelters were located on reserves and served an exclusively indigenous population. Shelters in rural and remote areas generally offered a narrower range of services than urban facilities, and a greater proportion focused on short-stay crisis intervention. Reports indicated shortages of shelter spaces, trained staff, counseling, and access to affordable second-stage housing. These shortages impeded women from leaving abusive relationships.

Police received training in treating domestic violence victims, and agencies provided hotlines to report abuse. The government's Family Violence Initiative involved 15 federal departments, agencies, and crown corporations, including Status of Women Canada, Health Canada, and Justice Canada. These entities worked with civil society organizations to eliminate violence against women and advance women's human rights. Provincial and municipal governments also sought to address violence against women, often in partnership with civil society, including funding public education programs and services, hotlines, and shelters.

Female Genital Mutilation/Cutting (FGM/C): The law prohibits FGM/C for women and girls and prosecutes the offense as aggravated assault with a maximum penalty of 14 years' imprisonment. Persons committing or aiding another person to commit the offense may be charged with criminal negligence causing bodily harm (maximum penalty of 10 years' imprisonment) or criminal negligence causing death (maximum penalty of life imprisonment). Persons convicted of removing or assisting the removal of a child who is ordinarily a resident in Canada for the purpose of having FGM/C performed on the child face a maximum penalty of five years' imprisonment. Refugee status may be granted on the grounds of threatened FGM/C that may be considered gender-related persecution. Provincial child protection authorities may intervene to remove children from their homes if they are suspected to be at risk of FGM/C.

Although reliable statistics were not available, anecdotal evidence suggested some families from immigrant communities in which FGM/C is culturally accepted send their daughters abroad to have the procedure performed.

Other Harmful Traditional Practices: The criminal code does not specifically refer to "honor" killings, but it prosecutes such cases as murder. Murder convictions in the first or second degree carry minimum penalties of life imprisonment with eligibility for parole. The law limits the defense of "provocation" to prevent its application to cases of "honor" killing and cases of spousal homicide. The government enforced the law effectively. The government's citizenship guide for new immigrants explicitly states "honor" killings and gender-based violence carry severe legal penalties. The government trains law enforcement officials on issues of "honor"-based violence and maintains an interdepartmental working group focusing on forced marriage and "honor"-based violence.

In February, British Columbia's Supreme Court rejected the government's request to extradite a man and woman wanted in India on charges they allegedly ordered the "honor" killing of the woman's daughter there in 2000. The court found the relatives' human rights could be abused in India and urged the government to consider trying the couple in Canada. In August the Supreme Court of Canada agreed to hear an appeal of the case.

Sexual Harassment: The law does not contain a specific offense of "sexual harassment" but criminalizes harassment (defined as stalking), punishable by up to 10 years' imprisonment, and sexual assault, with penalties ranging from 10 years for nonaggravated sexual assault to life imprisonment for aggravated sexual assault. The government generally enforced these prohibitions. Federal and provincial labor standards laws provide some protection against harassment, and federal, provincial, and territorial human rights commissions have responsibility for investigating and resolving harassment complaints. Employers, companies, unions, educational facilities, professional bodies, and other institutions have internal policies against sexual harassment, and federal and provincial governments provide public education and advice.

Reproductive Rights: Couples and individuals have the right to decide the number, spacing, and timing of their children; manage their reproductive health; and have access to the information and means to do so, free from discrimination, coercion, or violence.

Discrimination: Women have the same legal status and rights in the judicial system as men, and the government enforced the rights effectively. Women were well represented in the labor force, including business and the professions. Credible sources reported women experienced some economic discrimination in terms of employment, credit, or pay equity for substantially similar work, or in owning or managing businesses, education, and housing. Labor groups reported women were underrepresented in executive positions in the private sector. A 2014 study by the Peterson Institute found women accounted for 7 percent of corporate board members, 14 percent of executives, 3 percent of chief executive officers, and 2 percent of board chairpersons at 2,074 Canadian companies surveyed. Seven provinces and two territories require private-sector companies to report annually on their efforts to increase the number of women appointed to executive corporate boards. The government's statistical agency reported that hourly wages for women were, on average, lower than for men but that the wage gap had narrowed over the past two decades.

Indigenous women living on reserves (where land is held communally) have matrimonial property rights. First Nations may choose to follow federal law or enact their own rules related to matrimonial real property rights and interests that respect their customs. Although these laws provide some legal protection, civil society organizations argued First Nations communities needed more resources for policing, shelters, family support, training, and capacity building to implement the laws effectively and enable better access to the justice system.

Indigenous women and men living on reserves are subject to the Indian Act, which defines status for the purposes of determining entitlement to a range of legislated rights and eligibility for federal programs and services. Indigenous women do not enjoy equal rights with indigenous men to transmit officially recognized status to their descendants.

Children

Birth Registration: Citizenship is derived both by birth within the country's territory and from one's parents. Births are registered immediately, and there were no reports of the government denying public services, such as education or health care, to those who failed to register.

Child Abuse: In 2014 (the latest available figures), the government's statistical agency recorded that 53,600 children and youth were victims of police-reported violent crime. The law criminalizes violence and abuse against children, including assault, sexual exploitation, child pornography, abandonment, emotional maltreatment, and neglect. Provincial and territorial child welfare services investigate cases of suspected child abuse and may provide counseling and other support services to families, or place children in child welfare care, where warranted. The federal Family Violence Initiative promotes awareness of family violence; works with research and community organizations to strengthen the capacity of criminal justice, housing, and health systems to respond to family violence; and supports data collection and research. Provincial and territorial governments also provide public education and prevention services, often in partnership with civil society.

Early and Forced Marriage: The law establishes 16 years as the legal minimum age of marriage. Data on the rate of marriage for individuals younger than 18 were unavailable, but early marriages were not known to be a major problem. The law criminalizes the removal of a child from the country for the purpose of early and forced marriage and provides for court-ordered peace bonds, which may include surrendering of a passport, to disrupt an attempt to remove a child for that purpose.

Female Genital Mutilation/Cutting (FGM/C): See Women above.

Sexual Exploitation of Children: The law prohibits the commercial sexual exploitation of children, the sale of children, and offering or procuring a child for child prostitution. Authorities enforced the law effectively. The minimum age of consensual sex is 16 years. Persons convicted of living off the proceeds of prostitution of a child younger than 18 face between two and 14 years' imprisonment. Persons who aid, counsel, compel, use, or threaten to use violence, intimidation, or coercion in relation to a child younger than 18 engaging in prostitution face between five and 14 years' imprisonment. Persons who solicit or obtain the sexual services of a child younger than 18 face between six months' and five years' imprisonment. Children, principally teenage females, were exploited in sex trafficking.

The law prohibits accessing, producing, distributing, and possessing child pornography. Maximum penalties range from 18 months' imprisonment for summary offenses to 10 years' imprisonment for indictable offenses.

International Child Abductions: The country is a party to the 1980 Hague Convention on the Civil Aspects of International Child Abduction. See the Department of State's *Annual Report on International Parental Child Abduction* report on compliance at travel.state.gov/content/childabduction/en/legal/compliance.html.

Anti-Semitism

Approximately 1 percent of the population is Jewish.

The B'nai Brith Canada League for Human Rights received 1,277 reports of anti-Semitic incidents in 2015, down 22 percent from 2014. More than half of the reports (914) came from the province of Ontario. Reports in 2015 included harassment (1,123 incidents, a decrease); vandalism, including graffiti; attacks on synagogues, private homes, community centers and property and desecration of cemeteries (136 incidents, a decrease); and violence against persons (10 incidents, a decrease). Some university students reported anti-Semitic attacks on campus. For example, in March unknown vandals painted graffiti in a bathroom at York University's Keele Campus.

Trafficking in Persons

See the Department of State's *Trafficking in Persons Report* at
www.state.gov/j/tip/rls/tiprpt/.

Persons with Disabilities

The constitution and law prohibit discrimination against persons with physical,
sensory, intellectual, and mental disabilities in employment, education, air travel
and other transportation, access to health care, the judicial system, or the provision
of other state services, and the government effectively enforced these prohibitions.
The federal minister of families, children, and social development, supported by
the minister of persons with disabilities, provides federal leadership on protecting
the rights of persons with disabilities, and provincial governments also have
ministerial-level representation. Federal and provincial governments effectively
implemented laws and programs mandating access to buildings, information, and
communications for persons with disabilities, but regulation varies by jurisdiction,
and there is no comprehensive federal legislation that protects the rights of persons
with disabilities.

Children with disabilities attended primary, secondary, and higher education, and
the majority attended classes with nondisabled peers or a combination of
nondisabled and special education classes with parental consent. Disparities in
educational access for students with disabilities existed between provinces and
among school boards within provinces. Policy differences included types of
services, criteria to determine eligibility, allocation of resources, access to
inclusive versus segregated classes or facilities, and the number of teachers,
teacher's aides, and therapists.

Disability rights nongovernmental organizations (NGOs) reported that persons
with disabilities experienced higher rates of unemployment and underemployment,
lower rates of job retention, and higher rates of poverty and economic
marginalization than the broader population.

Federal and provincial human rights commissions protected and promoted respect
for the rights of persons with disabilities. The government provided services and
monetary benefits, but disability groups noted a lack of coordination among
services. Facilities existed to provide support for persons with mental health
disabilities, but mental disability advocates asserted that the prison system was not

sufficiently equipped or staffed to provide the care necessary for those in the criminal justice system, resulting in cases of segregation and self-harm.

National/Racial/Ethnic Minorities

According to the government statistical agency, 1,295 incidents of hate crimes were reported to police in 2014, of which 611 were motivated by race or ethnic bias. Blacks constituted the most commonly targeted racial group, accounting for 238 incidents, and Jews 213. A detailed breakdown of victims of hate crime incidents by ethnic origin (except black and Jewish) was not available. The proportion of hate crimes involving violence, including assault and uttering threats, totaled 304 incidents.

The law prohibits discrimination on the basis of race. Federal, provincial, and territorial human rights commissions investigate complaints and raise public awareness. The federal Canadian Race Relations Foundation coordinates and facilitates public education and research and develops recommendations to eliminate racism and promote harmonious race relations.

Throughout the year activists led protests and sit-ins to denounce what they claimed was systemic racism by police forces. The protests followed police shootings of civilians and other events, including the July death in custody of a Somali Canadian in Ottawa. Police opened an investigation into the fatality.

Indigenous People

Indigenous people constituted approximately 4 percent of the national population and higher percentages in the country's three territories: Yukon, 23 percent; Northwest Territories, 52 percent; and Nunavut, 86 percent. Disputes over land claims, self-government, treaty rights, taxation, duty-free imports, fishing and hunting rights, and alleged police harassment were sources of tension. Indigenous people remained underrepresented in the workforce; overrepresented on welfare rolls and in prison populations; and more susceptible than other groups to suicide, poverty, chronic health conditions, and sexual violence. According to the government statistical agency, the overall violent victimization rate (which includes sexual assault, assault, and robbery) for indigenous persons in 2014 was 163 incidents per 1,000 people, more than double the rate of 74 incidents per 1,000 among nonindigenous persons. The rates of sexual assault and of spousal violence were almost three times higher than those of nonindigenous persons, and 51 percent of indigenous victims of spousal violence reported more severe forms of violence, compared with 23 percent of nonindigenous victims of spousal violence.

The law recognizes individuals registered under the Indian Act based on indigenous lineage and membership in a recognized First Nation as Status Indians, which confers eligibility to a range of federal services and programs. Status and services are withheld from unregistered or non-Status indigenous persons who do not meet eligibility criteria for official recognition or who may have lost status through marriage to a nonindigenous person or other disenfranchisement. According to the government statistical agency, indigenous children accounted for almost 50 percent of the approximately 30,000 children younger than 14 in foster care in 2011.

The law recognizes and specifically protects indigenous rights, including rights established by historical land claims settlements. Treaties with indigenous groups form the basis for the government's policies in the eastern part of the country, but there were legal challenges to the government's interpretation and implementation of treaty rights. Indigenous groups in the western part of the country that had never signed treaties continued to claim land and resources, and many continued to seek legal resolution of outstanding issues. As a result, the evolution of the government's policy toward indigenous rights, particularly land claims, depended on negotiation or legal challenges. As of 2014, the latest year for which statistics are available, approximately 385 unresolved specific claims or grievances filed by indigenous people regarding the implementation of treaties remained under assessment or in negotiation (not including claims in litigation or before the Specific Claims Tribunal, which is a judicial panel), according to government reports. As of 2014 the government reported that negotiations for 100 self-government and comprehensive land claims were active. Indigenous groups who cannot settle specific claims through negotiation within three years may refer the claim to the Specific Claims Tribunal or the courts for a decision.

The law imposes statutory, contractual, and common-law obligations to consult with indigenous peoples in the development and exploitation of natural resources on land covered by treaty or subject to land claims. According to a Supreme Court ruling, the federal government has the constitutional duty to consult and, where appropriate, accommodate indigenous peoples when the government contemplates actions that may adversely affect potential or established indigenous and treaty rights.

The Supreme Court has affirmed that indigenous title extends to territory used by indigenous peoples for hunting, fishing, and other activities prior to contact with Europeans, as well as to settlement sites. Provincial and federal governments may develop natural resources on land subject to indigenous title but are obliged to obtain consent of the indigenous titleholders in addition to existing constitutional duties to consult, and where necessary, accommodate indigenous peoples in matters that affect their rights. If governments cannot obtain consent, they may proceed with resource development only on the basis of a "compelling and substantial objective" in the public interest, in which the public interest is proportionate to any adverse effect on indigenous interests. The court has established that indigenous titles are collective in nature.

In 2015 the federally commissioned TRC on Indian Residential Schools released its full report and recommendations regarding allegations of abuse of indigenous children in residential schools. In May the federal government implemented one of the TRC's recommendations and settled a lawsuit for C$50 million ($38.4 million) with students the government placed at residential schools in Newfoundland and Labrador.

In January the Canadian Human Rights Tribunal ruled the federal government discriminated against indigenous children when it failed to fund welfare services for children living on reserves at the same level of services for off-reserve populations. In September the tribunal issued its second of two subsequent rulings ordering the government to comply and to provide information on how it was implementing the ruling.

In April the Supreme Court ruled unanimously the Metis (descendants of historical unions between indigenous and European persons) and non-Status Indians are Indians under the Constitution Act and fall under the jurisdiction of the federal government. Nearly 600,000 Canadians identify as Metis. Lack of clarity in law as to whether federal or provincial governments had jurisdiction with regard to Metis persons had inhibited negotiations, but the ruling clears the way for Metis and non-Status Indians to negotiate with the federal government on issues that could include land claims, government services, and hunting and trapping rights.

In July the government committed C$9 million ($6.9 million) to support implementation of the country's first national Inuit suicide-prevention strategy. The Inuit Tapiriit Kanatami, a national advocacy organization, drafted the plan.

In August an Ontario judge heard plaintiffs' arguments on a suit filed in 2009 by indigenous children involved in the "Sixties Scoop." The Scoop involved an estimated 20,000 indigenous children, 16,000 of them in Ontario, whom child welfare services removed from their parents' custody and placed with nonindigenous foster families in Canada and the United States. A separate group of plaintiffs filed a suit in Saskatchewan during the year on the same issue. Plaintiffs demanded compensation for emotional trauma and loss of culture. The government argued it acted in the best interests of the children and within social norms of the time. The trial on the Ontario suit was set to resume in December.

Acts of Violence, Discrimination, and Other Abuses Based on Sexual Orientation and Gender Identity

The law prohibits discrimination based on sexual orientation, and the criminal code provides penalties for crimes motivated by bias, prejudice, or hate based on personal characteristics, including sexual orientation. Manitoba, Saskatchewan, and the Northwest Territories explicitly prohibit discrimination on the basis of gender identity. Ontario, Nova Scotia, Prince Edward Island, Alberta, Newfoundland and Labrador, and British Columbia prohibit discrimination on the basis of gender identity and gender expression. New Brunswick, Quebec, and the Nunavut and Yukon territories prohibit such discrimination implicitly on the basis of "sex" or "gender."

Birth certificates issued by provinces and territories provide the basis of identification for legal documents, and procedures vary for changing legal gender markers to match an individual's outward appearance or chosen gender expression.

Provinces and territories have different requirements for persons to change their legal gender marker in documents such as birth certificates and identifications. Some provinces require one or more physicians to certify the applicant has completed gender reassignment surgery before an applicant may change the legal gender marker. The provincial governments of Newfoundland and Labrador, Prince Edward Island, Nova Scotia, British Columbia, Ontario, Saskatchewan, Manitoba, and Alberta allow residents to change their gender marker with a personal and/or physician's declaration indicating the individual's gender identity.

There were occasions of violence and abuse against individuals based on sexual orientation, but in general the government effectively implemented the law criminalizing such behavior. NGOs reported that stigma or intimidation was a known or likely factor in the underreporting of incidents of abuse. Some police forces employed liaison officers to the lesbian, gay, bisexual, transsexual, and intersex communities. In 2014, the last year for which data was available, the government's statistical agency reported that 155 of 1,295 police-reported hate crime incidents nationally were motivated by sexual orientation.

In May an arsonist attempted to burn down Montreal's Metropolitan Surgery Center, the only clinic in the country that offers surgery to create male or female genitals for transgendered patients. Montreal police were investigating the arson as a hate crime.

In June the government of Ontario announced it would no longer include gender designation on provincial health cards. The government also announced that in 2017 driver's license holders would be allowed the option of displaying an "X" on their card if they do not exclusively identify as male or female.

Other Societal Violence or Discrimination

There were reports of societal violence and discrimination against members of other minority, racial, and religious groups, but the government generally implemented the law criminalizing such behavior effectively.

In January an assailant attacked a group of Syrian refugees who had attended an event organized by an Islamic group in Vancouver. The assailant pepper-sprayed a group of migrants who were standing outside the venue. Police were investigating the incident as a hate crime.

Section 7. Worker Rights

a. Freedom of Association and the Right to Collective Bargaining

Federal and some provincial laws, including related regulations and statutory instruments, provide for the right of workers in both the public and the private sectors to form and join independent unions, conduct legal strikes, and bargain collectively. Workers in the public sector who provide essential services, including police and armed forces, do not have the right to strike but have mechanisms to provide for due process and to protect workers' rights. Workers in essential services had recourse to binding arbitration if labor negotiations failed. The law prohibits antiunion discrimination and provides for reinstatement of workers fired for union activity. There were no reports of antiunion discrimination or other forms of employer interference in union functions.

Federal labor law applies in federally regulated sectors, which include industries of extra-provincial or international character, transportation and transportation infrastructure that crosses provincial and international borders, marine shipping, port and ferry services, air transportation and airports, pipelines, telecommunications, banks, grain elevators, uranium mining and processing, works designated by the federal parliament affecting two or more provinces, protection of fisheries as a natural resource, many First Nation activities, and most crown corporations. These industries employed approximately 10 percent of workers.

The law grants the government exclusive authority to designate which federal employees provide an essential service and do not have the right to strike. The law also makes it illegal for an entire bargaining unit to strike if the government deems 80 percent or more of the employees of the unit essential.

Provincial and territorial governments regulate and are responsible for enforcing their own labor laws in all occupations and workplaces that are not federally regulated, leaving categories of workers excluded from statutory protection of freedom of association in several provinces. Some provinces restrict the right to strike. For example, agricultural workers in Alberta, Ontario, and New Brunswick do not have the right to organize or bargain collectively under provincial law.

The government effectively enforced applicable laws and regulations in a timely fashion, including with effective remedies and penalties such as corrective workplace practices and criminal prosecution for noncompliance and willful violations, and generally respected freedom of association and the right of collective bargaining in practice. Penalties were sufficient to deter violations. Administrative and judicial procedures were not subject to lengthy delays and appeals.

In 2014 public-service unions initiated legal action claiming the government's decision to limit the number of federal workers who can strike, contravened International Labor Organization conventions. In June the unions paused the suit after the government announced it planned to repeal the legislation.

The public-service unions suspended a suit challenging the government's decision to impose a rule allowing it to override contracts and impose changes to negotiated sick leave plans for the federal public service without negotiation. Federal public-service unions had filed suit against the government and sought an injunction to prevent unilateral imposition of a new sick leave plan but agreed to suspend the injunction application pending changes to the law.

b. Prohibition of Forced or Compulsory Labor

The law prohibits all forms of forced or compulsory labor, and the government effectively enforced the law. The law prescribes penalties for violations of up to 14 years' imprisonment, or life imprisonment in the case of certain aggravating factors, such as kidnapping or sexual assault. Such penalties were sufficiently stringent. During the year the government investigated and prosecuted cases of forced labor and domestic servitude.

The federal government held employers of foreign workers accountable by verifying employers' ability to pay wages and provide accommodation and, through periodic inspections and mandatory compliance reviews, ensuring that employers provided substantially the same wages, living conditions, and occupation specified in the employers' original job offer. The government can deny noncompliant employers permits to recruit foreign workers for two years and impose fines of up to C$100,000 ($76,400) per violation for employer abuses of the program. Some provincial governments imposed licensing and registration requirements on recruiters or employers of foreign workers and prohibited the charging of recruitment fees to workers.

There were reports that employers subjected noncitizen or foreign-born men and women to forced labor in the agricultural sector, food processing, cleaning services, hospitality, construction industries, and in domestic service. NGOs reported that bonded labor, particularly in the construction industry, and domestic servitude constituted the majority of cases of forced labor.

Also see the Department of State's *Trafficking in Persons Report* at www.state.gov/j/tip/rls/tiprpt/.

c. Prohibition of Child Labor and Minimum Age for Employment

There is no federal minimum age for employment. In federally regulated sectors, children younger than 17 may work only when they are not required to attend school under provincial legislation, provided the work does not fall under excluded categories (such as work underground in a mine, on a vessel, or in the vicinity of explosives), and the work does not endanger health and safety. Children may not work in any federally regulated sector between the hours of 11 p.m. and 6 a.m.

The provinces and territories have primary responsibility for regulation of child labor, and minimum age restrictions vary by province. Regulation occurs across a range of laws including employment standards, occupational health and safety, education laws, and in regulations for vocational training, child welfare, and licensing of establishments for the sale of alcohol. Most provinces restrict the number of hours of work to two or three hours on a school day and eight hours on a nonschool day and prohibit children ages 12 to 16 from working without parental consent, after 11 p.m., or in any hazardous employment.

Authorities effectively enforced child labor laws and policies, and federal and provincial labor ministries carried out child labor inspections either proactively or in response to formal complaints. There were reports that limited resources hampered inspection and enforcement efforts. Penalties were pecuniary and varied according to the gravity of the offense.

There were reports that child labor occurred, particularly in the agricultural sector. There were also reports that children, principally teenage females, were subjected to sex trafficking and commercial sexual exploitation (see section 6, Children).

d. Discrimination with Respect to Employment and Occupation

The law and regulations prohibit discrimination with respect to employment or occupation on the basis of race, color, sex, religion, national origin or citizenship, disability, sexual orientation and/or gender identity, age, language, HIV-positive status, or other communicable diseases. Some provinces, including Quebec, New Brunswick, and Newfoundland and Labrador, as well as the Northwest Territories, prohibit employment discrimination on the grounds of social origin, "social condition," or political opinion. Federal law requires equal pay for equal work for four designated groups in federally regulated industries enforced through the Canadian Human Rights Commission on a complaint basis: women, persons with disabilities, indigenous persons, and visible minorities. Ontario and Quebec have pay equity laws that cover both the public and private sectors, and other provinces require pay equity only in the public sector.

Authorities encouraged individuals to resolve employment-related discrimination complaints through internal workplace dispute resolution processes as a first recourse, but federal and provincial human rights commissions investigated and mediated complaints and enforced the law and regulations. The government enforced the law effectively, but some critics complained that the process was complex and failed to issue rulings in a timely manner. Foreign migrant workers have the same labor rights as citizens and permanent residents, although NGOs alleged that discrimination occurred against migrant workers.

e. Acceptable Conditions of Work

Provincial and territorial minimum wage rates ranged from C$10.45 to C$13.00 ($7.91 to $9.84) per hour as of May. There is no official poverty income level. Some provinces exempt agricultural, hospitality, and other specific categories of workers from minimum wage rates. For example, Ontario has a minimum wage for persons younger than 18 who work less than 28 hours per week when school is in session, at a rate lower than the respective minimum for adult workers.

Standard work hours vary by province, but in each the limit is 40 or 48 hours per week, with at least 24 hours of rest. The law requires payment of a premium for work above the standard workweek. Entitlement to paid annual leave varies by province, but the law requires a minimum of 10 days' paid annual leave per year (or payment of 4 percent of wages in lieu) after one year of continuous employment. Some provinces mandate an additional week of paid leave to employees who have completed a specified length of service. There is no specific prohibition on excessive compulsory overtime, which is regulated by means of the required rest periods in the labor code that differ by industry. Some categories of workers have specific employment rights that differ from the standard, including commercial fishermen, oil field workers, loggers, home caregivers, professionals, managers, and some sales staff.

Federal law provides safety and health standards for employees under federal jurisdiction. Provincial and territorial legislation provides for all other employees, including foreign and migrant workers. Standards were current and appropriate for the industries they covered. Federal, provincial, and territorial laws protect the right of workers with "reasonable cause" to refuse dangerous work and remove themselves from hazardous work conditions, and authorities effectively enforced this right. The government also promoted safe working practices and provided training, education, and resources through the Canadian Center for Occupational Health and Safety, a federal agency composed of representatives of government, employers, and labor.

Minimum wage, hours of work, and occupational health and safety standards were effectively enforced. Federal and provincial labor departments monitored and effectively enforced labor standards by conducting inspections through scheduled and unscheduled visits, in direct response to reported complaints, and at random.

Penalties were pecuniary and varied according to the gravity of the offense. Under the federal labor code, maximum penalties for criminal offenses, including criminal negligence causing death or bodily harm, or willful breach of labor standards in which the person in breach knew that serious injury or death was likely to occur, could include imprisonment. Enforcement measures include a graduated response, with a preference for resolution via voluntary compliance, negotiation, and education; prosecution and fines serve as a last resort. Some trade unions continued to note that limited resources hampered the government's inspection and enforcement efforts.

NGOs reported migrants, new immigrants, young workers, and the unskilled were vulnerable to violations of the law on minimum wage, overtime pay, unpaid wages, and excessive hours of work. NGOs also alleged that restrictions on the types of labor complaints accepted for investigation and delays in processing cases discouraged the filing of complaints.

According to the Association of Workers Compensation Boards of Canada, during 2014, the most recent year for which data were available, there were 919 workplace fatalities. During the year there were some reports of workplace accidents.

In January the Ontario Court of Appeal sentenced a Toronto project manager to three and one-half years in prison after a scaffolding collapse in 2009 killed four workers. The court also levied fines against the employer for failing to ensure the equipment was safe.

In September, Ontario's Ministry of Labor issued six health and safety violation orders against Toronto-based Fiera Foods following the death of a temporary worker crushed by machinery when her clothing became caught in a conveyer belt.